PEACE
BY
PEACE

99 steps toward violence prevention & de-escalation in everyday life

Ian Brennan

Peace by Peace: 99 steps toward violence prevention & de-escalation in everyday life
© 2025 Ian Brennan
This edition © 2025 PM Press

ISBN: 979-8-88744-088-0 (paperback)
ISBN: 979-8-88744-094-1 (ebook)
Library of Congress Control Number: 2024939655
Cover by John Yates / www.stealworks.com
Interior design by briandesign

10 9 8 7 6 5 4 3 2 1

PM Press
PO Box 23912
Oakland, CA 94623
www.pmpress.org

Printed in the USA.

Contents

Prologue   vii

Introduction   1

Modest Strain   5

99 steps toward violence prevention &
de-escalation   9

Epilogue   129

Afterword   133

Overviews   135

About the Author   141

This book by design is a quick read—quasi bullet points and tools to encapsulate larger concepts. It can be read either linearly or opened to any page. The emphasis is on management of one-on-one, interpersonal encounters.

Peace by Peace is intended for anyone and everyone, to be applied wherever people interact—home, work, throughout our daily lives, not just clinical environments.

Anyone desiring a more intensive exploration of these themes is kindly directed to my two previous books on the topic (*Anger Antidotes* and *Hate-less*), which number in the hundreds of pages. The goal here is to provide options and choice, not immutable formula.

With these topics, it is nearly a given that some of the material could be triggering, so please beware.

If ever it seems that I'm making fun of anybody, it is myself. The majority of errors explored here are ones that I've committed and probably will again someday—maybe even *tomorrow*—no matter how wholesome my wishes.

I am neither an extremist nor a centrist but a *spectrumist*. Total agreement with every idea by every reader is not the ambition but a communal and unending search for truth.

Prologue

On a plane home from the USA, for most of twelve hours a toddler wailed inconsolably. He was conducting an experiment: could he trust that help would surface when summoned?

The wordless answer was "no."

His burgeoning life bent on that arc. An experience destined not to be consciously remembered but nonetheless remain.

Prologue

Introduction

Peace begins with the acceptance of an imperfect world. Recognition of complex definitions rather than black-and-white labels is the starting point for progress.

Rather than overly simplistic claims like, "I'm not that kind of person," it is advisable to embrace that "Actually, I am *every* kind of person—both good and bad."

We live in fluid states along a continuum and are not exactly the same figure to any two people, in any two situations or even with the same individuals at different points in time.

We must resist the tendency to reduce others and experiences to all-or-nothing, either/or equations.

Further, it is imperative that we aspire to more than measuring ourselves against the worst. The Holocaust, Nazis, cannibals, KKK, child molesters, and serial killers are widely used counterexamples for our own shortcomings but hardly make healthy measures of morality.

Two media forces work in tandem to the detriment of our collective mental well-being:

1. The extreme, binary language used in the advertising and propaganda that we're bombarded with daily.
2. The celebration and modeling of reactive versus responsive behavior.

Instead, too often people's ambivalence is vilified. But ambivalence is precisely where much positive potential and redemption lie. Those at the extremes can rarely be stopped or dissuaded. But the majority of us stand teetering somewhere amid the span and can go either direction if encouraged or enabled.

What follows is founded on viewing violence as a last resort rather than an inevitability. But nothing herein is ever intended to assign any blame to victims or those who've chosen to act heroically in prevention of greater, emergent harm.

Having spent over thirty years teaching violence prevention, crisis resolution, and anger management, what follows are the core, consistent lessons that those years have provided. When speaking of violence, it is meant in all its variants—verbal, emotional, social, and physical.

I was first asked by supervisors to train fellow staff members after it was noticed that I'd demonstrated a particular facility with calming volatile situations. One coworker claimed that I "could talk down a rattlesnake." That being what it may, over time I was forced to come to terms with my own anger, camouflaged beneath a calm exterior.

The curriculum itself was hatched from working for fifteen years in locked, emergency psychiatric settings, mostly in Oakland, California. In those environments, utility was vital for survival. Mere theory would get your ass kicked. The techniques had to be effective or else immediate physical consequences could result. This risk was tragically proven by more than one colleague being killed on the job, countless assaulted, and some maimed.

The unexpected by-product and blessing of this work has been participants recurrently confiding how much these techniques have helped in their personal lives—with children, family, neighbors, or partners—as much as, if not more than, professionally.

This is not a self-help book, any more than *every* book is self-help. The objectives here are modest. If even one idea presented helps a single person live a tiny bit more peacefully, then the whole endeavor has been worthwhile.

The trajectory of my life was altered at age twenty-one by a sudden, heinous, and predatory act inflicted upon a loved one. Every person that moment reached was transfigured by it. The repercussions resound to this day.

Modest Strain

(meditations from a life spent on the psychiatric ward)

1969: My mother stood frozen behind the second-floor psychiatric ward window. Three years old, too young to visit a patient, I waved to her from the sidewalk below. She did not wave back.

At that moment, my professional destiny involuntarily sealed.

My first hospital job was changing diapers for minimum wage on the graveyard shift. We'd circle Pine Sol–soaked halls and, by the time our rounds were finished, be forced to return back where we'd started since those patients needed to be changed once again.

It was a backbreaking, poorly paying, and unsavory job that often encountered staffing shortages. Nonetheless, no hospital wanted to hire me. An adolescent male with heavy-metal hair was suspect.

My first night, a patient I'd changed just hours earlier passed. This was my initiation.

I'd crossed into a world of crisis.

In psychiatric hospitals, I was ultimately brought on as "muscle"—drafted as a member of the goon squad. But that role held little allure for me. Words possessed the real power.

Once I entered a patient dormitory room just as a young man the same age as me launched himself off a bedside table and began swinging from a noose he'd fashioned out of a sheet. I ran, and as trained encircled his legs in a bear hug and lifted, relieving the pressure on his neck. He went limp and survived.

But something in me gave way.

As the overweight brother of a sister with Down syndrome, I was exposed routinely to bullying. I moved to fists far too easily as a child, a norm in our working-class suburb.

But I am thankful to my classmate, Cesar, who bit me and nearly took a chunk out of my forearm as I pinned him to the ground, my weight double his. I retain gratitude to Russ, who was a head shorter than me, and whose father and older brothers battered him. He popped me in the mouth with brass knuckles, chipping my front tooth, as we circled each other. These were wake-up calls.

My second-to-last brawl took place in junior high metal shop. Another ostracized boy and I traded our wrath as we shuffled between buzzing circular saws and red-hot furnaces. The haggard and aged public school instructor barked and yanked us by our shirt collars to break it up. And that was the end. No being sent to the principal, no notice given to our parents.

Once again, we were left to fend for ourselves in the absence of emotional guidance.

I officially remained a "good" kid, a straight-A student. One who was allegedly not angry. My perfect record maintained.

When I was a small child in the seventies, my father had fits of road rage long before it'd been given a name. I would immediately look toward the people in the opposing car and try to imagine what they were feeling and thinking.

Usually, they were completely oblivious to his tirade. The remainder mirrored him—screaming and cursing even more vehemently, convinced it was they that'd been wronged. They too were held hostage by their own frustrations. Trapped within their steel-and-glass bubbles, they slid past.

Legally, whoever commands superior power possesses the greater responsibility—the bicyclist must yield to the pedestrian, the motorist to the cyclist. The challenge is to maintain the mindset of a pedestrian—even when behind the wheel of an eighteen-wheeler.

99 steps toward violence prevention & de-escalation

1

Self-control is ultimately a selfish action. Anger boomerangs.

a. Everyone is harmed by a violent act, including the aggressor (albeit usually to a lesser degree). Every person on every side of violence—any last person it touches—is diminished on some level.

2

Options are the crossroads of crisis. They present the path forward and away from helplessness.

Lacking choice, people grow desperate.

3

Choices should be provided in groups of three or more, never just two. This helps avoid the binary trap of ultimatums and false dichotomies.

a. Another beneficial aspect of this is that the third option need not be anything at all but simply indicated as possibly existing. What matters is the willingness to even consider and search for other possible solutions beyond the extremes and whatever is currently evident.

4

The single greatest self-defense maneuver in the world?

Walk away.

The one self-defense maneuver that you will always need?

RUN!

Never "stand your ground."

The safest and most economical self-defense method is that which is 100 percent focused on defense, sans retaliation.

a. Relatedly, let them talk, let them walk. Do not try to have the last word. Too many people's parting procla-mation on the planet is "Fuck you." It becomes their accidental epitaph. How much better if lives ended with "I love you."

b. The flip side of all this is that if we do *choose* to stand and fight for the protection of others or for a higher cause, that remains our personal liberty. But it's tomfoolery to do so without forethought and the assumption of full responsibility for whatever choice we make.

c. Sadly, many domestic disturbances arise from part-ners *following* each other, physically denying flight as an alternative to fighting, even after flight has been enacted.

d. We are the most intellectual animal but the dumbest in terms of survival. For unlike almost all other species, we remain in situations we could've escaped from but chose to stay—mostly due to ego and symbolism. Even worse, we often return after having safely escaped.

We are potentially willing to suffer physical death or injury rather than a narcissistic wound, to harm or kill others in attempts to protect or bolster our self-esteem.

e. Too often, self-defense *from ourselves* is what's needed most.

5

The first objective in any crisis situation is to not make it *worse*. If we are able to achieve that alone, we are doing worlds better than most.

Only once we've monitored that we haven't prompted any backsliding or undercutting can we begin trying to help improve things.

a. Any success in making progress will be dependent on our humility and readiness to accept that as much as we may desire, we still may not be able to fix every woe. Instead, solutions are almost always dependent on the other's receptivity and willingness to participate. Though we can perform impeccably and by the book, the outcome can still falter.

b. Beware that the most severe accidents tend to occur *amid* an existing accident, one that has been overcorrected or overreacted to.

c. Do not make situations life-or-death, unless they are the exceedingly rare cases that truly are life-or-death.

6

The greatest verbal skill is not to talk but listen.

a. Further, sometimes listening is the only viable option. The person speaking may only desire to be heard and not be amenable to listen to what anyone else has to say.

b. In truth, the more intense an issue is, the less we should say. But in these cases the urge is usually to do the contrary and say more. Yet almost nothing we can utter is powerful enough to ease profound pain. Believing otherwise is to operate from a self-centered conceit that's masterfully bound to inflict larger injury.

c. The aim is to listen to someone (nonverbally) even *when we are the one speaking.*

7

Appeal to the healthier aspects of an individual. This requires faith that every individual has goodness in them, however dim. There is more to every person than we can see. Our moral responsibility is to attempt to look beyond what is evident—toward the complexity and virtue within others. The objective is to peer past the armor of anger and the intoxication of the moment.

a. The tug-of-war we routinely face is that while we may be attempting to calm a situation, the other person is simultaneously working to provoke the unhealthier aspects in our person—the darker impulses. We can only hope to control these impulses in ourselves if we first acknowledge that they do indeed exist.

b. Rather than falling prey to the self-centeredness of paranoia, it's healthier to assume good intentions on the part of others. Even more realistically, most people simply have *no* intention toward us whatsoever. Though we are understandably our own focus, we rarely are anyone else's.

Far more than hostility, what we most often face is indifference. The majority of other people already possess far better targets to harm than us, so take care not to provide them with ammunition or justifications to turn toward us instead.

Paranoia is just another incarnation of grandiosity—the conviction that people even realize that you exist, let alone care enough to willfully harm you.

c. The provocateur's goal is for us to assume the role of the villain in a primordial script that justifies their behaving in ways that they wouldn't otherwise and, thus, relieves them of responsibility. Instead as a counterbalance, we can strive to be beyond reproach.

Almost every violent action is believed by the aggressor to be defensive or retaliatory—not offensive but principled.

d. Many people will fight more to defend others than themselves. Though some may even remain in abusive relationships, if you touch their kids or a puppy, they'll go berserk.

Almost everyone fights for the same basic reason—perceived injustice. Injustice is made clearer and almost undeniable when the violence is inflicted on a child or an aged, significantly smaller or disabled person. Building on those existing circles of care to expand and include almost every person—even those seemingly not as vulnerable—can make our communities more harmonious and charitable.

e. The ultimate double bind is those who play the victim *while* provoking—proclaiming peace while actually being on the attack. When operating from this manipulative and disingenuous pose, the net effect either way is a win to some degree for the perpetrator. The self-righteous are especially adept at this game.

Our culture has been twisted extensively to search more for fault than value in things, a by-product of a society where people have been fortified toward hypercompetitiveness.

8

Far from merely being politically correct mumbo-jumbo, words matter. This is because renaming precedes maiming.

a. In order for almost any intentional violence to occur, the aggressor must first view the victim as other, lesser, and deserving of harm—an object, subhuman. Instead, it's incredibly difficult to inflict willful harm toward someone we actively have empathy for.

b. Whether instantaneous or the result of a long-standing prejudice, this dehumanization virtually always prefigures an attack regardless of the chosen term: cockroach, rats, asshole, savages, immigrant, mosquito, et cetera. Prominent patterns of exactly such verbal recoding have historically been found prior to every recognized genocide.

c. Take care that how we define the world and others aligns with our deepest values.

9

Thoughts are crucial. They build the blueprints of action. Rather than believing that we are peaceful and kind in the abstract, monitoring that our words and ideation correspond with our intentions reaps greater benefit.

a. Don't feed our own fantasies or another's. Do not flirt with or prime ourselves for unwanted outcomes.
b. Observe that our thoughts reflect our beliefs and aspirations, and when they don't, actively interrupt indulging in preoccupations or fantasies that run opposite to our principles.
c. The lethal tipping point is from fantasizing about something to rehearsing and planning for that action.
d. Do not forearm for crimes that we never wish to perpetrate.

10

Ignore the behavior, not the individual.

a. Interrupt the urge to punish people for being unlikable or impoverished communicators.
b. Strive to be objective about their subjectivity.

11

Anger is symbolic and thought-generated. Most people are not truly mad but in despair. We "make" ourselves irate; anger is a self-inflicted wound.

a. Anger is a secondary emotion designed to protect the individual from their sense of vulnerability that has resulted from the primary, core emotions of fear, frustration, and sadness.

b. A shortcut to managing one's own anger is to cut straight to the sorrow that lies beneath rage. Get *sad*, not mad. Skip the intermediary protest and posturing step entirely. That is where most people get derailed or stuck.

c. An additional trick during a crisis is to immediately give thanks for matters not yet being so much worse than they could be and to recognize how fortunate we remain despite the current setbacks and frustrations.

12

We are actually engaging in fear management, not anger management. And that management is largely of people's fear of exposing their own fear—the fear *of* fear.

a. "Threatening people" are actually threatened. Their goal is to scare others enough to goad them into expressing the fear that the perpetrators themselves are afraid to express.
b. In fact, almost all disagreeable behaviors—controlling, defensive, judgmental—are underpinned by the actor's shrouded anxiety.

13

Being aware of what we feel is additionally vital because it's among the best gauges for what the other person is feeling.

a.   If they make us afraid, they are afraid. If we feel frustrated in their presence, so are they. And unhappy people are generally driven—consciously or unconsciously—to bring everyone around them down.

14

We do not get anger "out of our system." It only intensifies due to the underlying emotions not being recognized and processed.

a.   Further, the angrier we become, the more we encounter anger from others—whether their counterresponses are immediate or delayed. The episodes where postponements occur simply represent a false peace, retribution deferred.

b.   Energy doesn't "go away." It goes *somewhere*.

c.   Anger is generally passed down by the back of the hand, the volume of the voice, or both.

d.   When people act as cheerleaders for a friend's anger, they mistake that they are being supportive of that individual. In fact, they are not being supportive of the person but of *that person's fury*. Beware especially those who vicariously get others to act out for them—sexually, aggressively, or through gluttony. Parental figures are especially prone to doing so.

e.   Behavioral incontinence is found in those who seem to have never met an impulse they didn't like, a stimulus that they could deny or ignore.

     The opposite of this is emotional continence. This is not advocacy for stoicism but instead for deeper passion. Passion that remains within our control due to our remaining highly sensitized to our feelings and those around us.

15

Our concern should not be with the intentions of another's cold self but their conduct in the heat of the moment. Every individual behaves adequately some, if not much, of the time.

a.   Therefore, the focus is not how a person relates at their best but how they function under stress—their dynamic energy. Not the strength of a building at rest but during a 6.8 earthquake. Not the composure of a person just awakening after a long night's rest but when they're sleep-deprived, haven't eaten since Thursday, and just downed a fifth of Jack Daniels.

16

Most conflict is confusion—an escalated lack of under-standing. The misapprehension that the other person is thoroughly unredeemable.

a. Rather than only offering empathy exclusively to a
    few select others it should be taken as a given that all
    people, no matter how unsavory, are operating from
    unprocessed pain.

17

Revenge is asymmetrical.

a. Escalation results from one party doing something worse to the other than what was done to them. Therefore, it is *not* actually an "eye for an eye," as is commonly claimed, but a *head* for an eye.
b. One person may have started it. But two or more people almost always finish it. Attempts to "even the score" invariably result in contests of one-upmanship.
c. Nearly all unhealthy relationships share this sort of imbalance. People then shrink or inflate to fit the available space.

18

Our goal is to break the instinctual, social pattern of reciprocity and engage instead in noncomplementary behavior. In prosocial interactions, reciprocity is routine (e.g., a smile for a smile), but it worsens matters when brought to antisocial or asocial encounters.

Remaining calm is not be to confused with apathy. Calmness instead is founded on being acutely aware of how we feel but without being ruled by those emotions.

a. The provoker is attempting to enlist you as a collaborator, issuing an invitation to become their chosen, antagonistic partner in a mutually destructive caper.

b. And whenever we become the enemy, the instigator is victorious. Violence has not been eradicated due to our retaliation but rather duplicated and amplified. The bedrock struggle is whether we become more like them or they like us.

c. An oft-overlooked element is that violent encounters are charged with intimacy as they likely carry ineffable outcomes for both parties that would not have otherwise occurred. Often a complete stranger instantly becomes the most significant actor in the course of a person's life, and possibly the last person they'll ever interact with.

d. What we are engaging in is a short-term interpersonal loan, not a permanent contortion. We're modeling the behavior we hope that they will adopt so that healthier boundaries can be established or restored.

e. Much power is derived from self-control since it stands in dramatic relief to the low bar that most capitalist societies have set. Large numbers of citizens have been conditioned to reflexive behavior versus introspection, and are pathetically willing to throw down at a moment's notice.

Starting a fight is hardly an accomplishment. Halting one is.

19

Opportunity dictates action.

a. Environments are not behaviorally neutral. Instead, behavior is largely situation-dependent (e.g., it is impossible to stab someone with a knife if no knife is present).

b. Thus, those who arm themselves in advance with weapons or words are only contingently peaceful, and they become increasingly milieu-dependent as to which behaviors are acceptable. This causes them to grow fearful since the external world then acts as dictator and puppeteer for that person's own actions, particularly any time things don't go as planned.

20

People unwittingly prime themselves for negative behavior through self-permission and mental preparations.

A central question is: What are our preparations? For peace or war.

It is these cultivations which are enacted at a moment's peak stress—the subtext.

a. One of the best ways to be proactive regarding crisis is to never authorize in advance *any* breaking-point where unacceptable behaviors become acceptable—to dispose of the "ifs" and "buts" clauses.

b. If we sincerely desire peace, we are called upon to purify ourselves ongoingly by exploring our own triggers and committing in advance to not allowing these elements to alter our conduct dramatically.

c. The bulk of the toil in crisis resolution occurs beforehand—prepping oneself on how to respond versus react. It's as if we are training for a race that we hope we're never called upon to run but that could start at any moment.

d. A key is to establish a ceiling on our own escalations that is not to be exceeded regardless of whatever is the matter at hand (barring truly dire physical danger).

   My father was a locomotive engineer. He taught me on steep grades to use the motor itself to the slow the descent, not the brakes—to shift down to a lower gear and stay there until you reached the bottom.

e. Practice patience by viewing minor frustrations as emotional "workouts" and blessings that can strengthen us for the larger tests that undoubtedly lie ahead.

f. More than touchy-feely, "living in the present," it's better to resist becoming drunk with the moment. The attempt is to inhabit the now while simultaneously conducting cost analysis that eyes a better and sustainable future.

g. Much aggression arises not from historically violent individuals but from the *tentatively* "nonviolent"—those who may not have previously externalized violence but internally were rehearsing such actions and harboring grudges daily for years or decades, whether intentionally or unintentionally. Internally, they built a nuclear bomb—often designed for those dearest to them—rather than burying that technology, never to be found again.

h. In relationships, choose to not keep score (or groom ourselves for combat).

21

Perfectionism is the enemy of progress.

a. Our focus is better placed on progress versus perfection—the acknowledgment of how things *are* versus how they *should* be.

b. What might merely be average behavior for most adults could still be monumental for an individual who is struggling to change and improve.

c. Perfectionism leads to puritanism whereby any imperfection is seen as intolerable rather than quite typical. And whenever all nuance is lost, anything on the negative spectrum becomes catastrophic, intolerable, and virtually indistinguishable. This is our cultural legacy, one of damnation. Within this paradigm, personal errors incite terror since they become unforgivable rather than being viewed more kindly as inevitable.

   When a person announces, "I'm not prejudiced," what they're really divulging is, "I *try* not to be and wish I wasn't."

d. The goal is not to fix universally innate societal ills but to improve them proportionately. These are generational works, not occasions.

e. Just as much as—if not more than—progress, we need to first invest in maintenance to prevent regression. Murder, rape, assault, and theft sadly have always been with us, and tragically always will be to some degree. No society is without them, no people have found a cure. Instead, minimizing their occurrences and ensuring that we do not unintentionally promote or normalize them is a more realistic investment.

22

Ego is the root of nearly all evil.

a. Therefore, acceptance of our own faults and limitations must be admitted ... though, not celebrated either. For, "I am the *worst*," is just the incognito twin of self-aggrandizement.

b. Most encounters escalate when the focus shifts from task-orientation to self-orientation. Thus, those with chronic self-focus are most conflict prone to begin with.

c. Somewhat counterintuitively, excellent peacemakers are often the ones who doubt their abilities most.

d. Be wary not just of obviously arrogant or narcissistic behaviors but also the softer forms as well—such as individuals that are rigidly cheery, unresponsive to context and their current circumstances.

e. Use of the inclusive words "us" and "we" helps heal the divide of the "you/I" split. When we refer to "I/me/mine" it indicates opposition and the extremities of right/wrong, winner/loser. Instead, "we/us" offer alignment.

f. "Let's" is especially potent as it centers optimistically on the future while also skipping self-reference and divisive "yes/no questions" entirely.

g. All of these unifying terms operate hypnotically, bypassing the receiver's negative judgments so that purer information can potentially be received.

h.   The largest bait that people use to provoke emotions in others—both negative and positive—is the word "you." Almost nothing triggers pride and self-interest more reliably. That is why "you" is the hallmark of propagandists, pop songwriters, salespeople, manipulators, intimidators, and other provocateurs. Unless its use is deliberate, avoidance of the "you" word is advisable. And hyperconsciousness of when it is spoken by others is imperative to maintaining our own composure and objectivity.

i.   It is not us versus them but us *with* us.

Only us.

All of us.

23

There is a vast difference between being a pacifist and being passive. The former is by choice, rather than determined by cowardice or defeat.

a. Ethical action is not a one-size-fits-all affair. It requires responding flexibility to each episode based on the specific dynamics involved.
b. The foundational measure of any action's effectiveness is whether it is having the desired impact. If not, then we should change course accordingly.

24

Past orientation acts as a primary impediment to seeking solutions. This is the space where many quarrels are summoned. Precedents are a major tripping point in managing conversations productively, and references to them rarely prove advantageous. Instead, they almost always raise ire and people's guard.

a. We must first allow them to grieve and mourn the loss of their ideal—what could've been or what they'd envisioned—before recalibrating and shifting their attention to alternative options and solutions.
b. Listen to the past, talk about the future.
c. Often conflicts arise over timeliness. In actuality, we can often give the person exactly what they want, just not *when* they want it. It is advisable to attempt refocusing on the future and that which is possible *eventually*, rather than what is being denied currently.

25

Being "crazy" is not talking to yourself so much as the *way* we talk to ourselves.

a. Our language is healthier when it is comprehensive of all possibility rather than rigidly restricting solutions or alternative actions to binary equations.

26

Decision making is largely an emotional rather than an intellectual process.

a. It is difficult to determine which is scarier—someone's ignorance or their intellect. Particularly, when that intellect—often of a superior level—is misused to support and sustain the individual's own emotional immaturity.

   Someone can be a great-grandmother, have a double PhD in psychology, and still be batshit crazy. (And the two-year-old in the family might be the most empathic and emotionally attuned of the whole bunch.)

b. The majority of us suffer from a sense of individual invincibility. Though we possess an intellectual understanding of risks, we nonetheless retain an emotional sense that the consequences somehow still don't apply to us.

c. As an example, there are few greater intellectual authorities on addiction than recovering addicts. They have thought about the issue more than others. But being able to speak about a subject versus applying that information in real time are two very different things. Attempting to talk someone out of dependance or a compulsion is akin to asking them to stop having blue eyes or being seven feet tall.

d. When I was growing up, a distant relative married a man who claimed that he didn't need to wear a seatbelt because if he was ever in an accident he'd just brace himself by gripping the steering wheel stoutly. He was a cerebrally educated man—an attorney—but a pair of broken thumbs and a busted nose from a minor fender-bender forced him to "feel" how preposterous his delusion had been (and also provided him an experiential lesson in basic physics).

27

Almost all problem behaviors arise from extremes—both the active extreme and its lesser-recognized, subtle shadow (e.g., not just the loud person but also the overly quiet one).

a. Most people don't ask for help but stay silent until they *scream* for it, long after the need is overdue.

b. So much ill behavior is born from the passive extreme, with people first resenting that they have to do *anything* at all. That is followed by tension building hydraulically—like a slingshot being pulled back— until the person snaps and explodes, often seemingly out of "nowhere."

c. Contrastingly, an individual who yells or threatens can often be worked with. Though feared and resented more, they are at least attempting to communicate and in their own ham-handed way are asking for help. It is those that refuse to acknowledge their difficultly or accept help, that are to be more greatly feared.

Some of the "nicest" people—the terminally chipper—are the least emotionally forthright.

28

An overriding danger is underestimation.

a. People are very rarely injured by individuals or in situations that they consider a risk or threat. For in those cases, their denial of danger is usually overcome, and at minimum the person tries to prevent catastrophic consequences, if possible.

b. It is not what we worry about that usually gets us but rather what we *don't* worry about.

c. From a strictly tactical safety standpoint, be concerned whenever someone carries themselves with an inexplicable confidence. There is likely something they know that we don't—that they are a skilled fighter, carrying a weapon, are an ambassador's nephew or have larger friends nearby.

d. Our unsubstantiated optimism or dismissiveness too often gets us harmed or killed. This is the Titanic syndrome—forgetting that nothing is unsinkable.

e. The practice is to weigh not just intention but also negligence—not only the active elements but also the passive. Few people have knowingly nefarious designs. But also rare are those who overcome their denial and laziness, and consistently address safety, rather than gambling with their own or others' safety.

I trust that most of the time almost no one

calculates harm, but that does little to impede a lack of due diligence from running epidemic.

f. The most supreme crisis resolution often acts invisibly and goes uncredited, as what would've resulted from its absence, instead, does not occur.
g. My goal is not to be lucky. The goal is to not be *un*lucky.
h. I operate from the assumption that everyone I meet can kick my ass. And I never want to find out that I am wrong.

Almost every "war story" I've heard over the years about staff injuries involves assaults from the elderly, wheelchair users, or petite people. If we treated everyone with the same basic respect afforded Mike Tyson or a grizzly bear, we'd rarely be caught unprepared.

29

We often conflate probability with possibility. An outcome may be more or less likely to occur but that doesn't eliminate the *possibility* of exceptions and surprises (e.g., although statistically men commit most physically violent actions throughout the world, that far from means that women cannot be violent as well).

a. Fear no one *and* everyone at the same time . . . at least a little bit.

    Whenever someone contends that they are "not afraid of *anybody*," rather than our displaying the admiration that's sought the sensible rejoinder is, "What's wrong with you?" Even an infant can be lethal if clasping a meat cleaver.

b. No culture or race has a monopoly or exemption from any behavior known to humankind. Madness, goodness, and posers are found everywhere on sliding scales from place to place and era to era.

c. Quest to not hold as proof the false negatives of what you've not witnessed, nor let the consequences that have not happened *yet* stand as evidence for a course of action's soundness (e.g., the vanity of "Well, it's never been a problem *for me*," or "We've always done it this way.").

d. Relatedly, consensus building and more logical conclusions are routinely derailed by the citation of the exceptional cases where things deviate from the norm. These are the "but couldn't" arguments.

Yes, something *could* prove true on rare occasion, but that hardly invalidates the more likely outcomes. When the sincere intention is constructiveness, balance and proportion are what weighs most substantially.

Just because something *can* potentially be the case in no sizable way reduces what is most *probable*.

30

The mere presence of an impulse is not usually the quandary. The inability to control the impulse is the crux of the matter.

a. Almost all of us have experienced aggressive, homicidal, suicidal, and self-destructive urges, no matter how fleeting.
b. The primitive, reptilian brain stem is triggered approximately three times more quickly than the higher-functioning frontal lobe. All of this occurs within less than a second. But in those fractions of a second, lives can change or even end. The body is constantly trying to race ahead of the mind and usurp it. The goal is to slow down the process and "think," to respond versus react.
c. In most aggressive actions, there is a decrease in rational thought which leads to a reduction in impulse control. If coupled with increased energy, this cocktail can be deadly. When under the influence of substances or emotion, our executive functioning declines. We cannot talk someone out of a physical basis for their behavior—such as alcohol or dementia. In those cases, attempts to de-escalate often instead exacerbate the situation.

    Generally, behavior arising from physical causes requires a physical intervention. For example, an inebriated person needs the time to detox before any tenable clarity can occur.

d. The knee-jerk question, "What was that person thinking?" can be answered easily, "They *weren't*." This is evidenced by drugs and alcohol being involved in the vast majority of the assaults, murders, and accidents that occur globally. The substances are not the cause of the behavior, but without a doubt help potentiate it.

e. What is often called the "fight-or-flight" reaction is actually "fight, flight, or *freeze*."

The overlooked aspect of victimization is shock. Often, individuals and onlookers were unable to respond in the moment due to being understandably overwhelmed.

31

Control your voice and you control yourself.

a. The objective measure of calmness is to speak more quietly than the person we are interacting with.
b. People first lose self-control vocally, then verbally, then physically. And when they attack, they usually stop talking entirely.
c. Therefore, the best way to get another person talking, keep them talking, and also to stimulate rational thought is to ask questions.
d. Vocal communication is not normally under our conscious control. When sounds are genuine, we do not *make* them, they happen. This is the case with sex, physical pain, humor, fright. Monitoring ourselves vocally is a specific way to exhibit serenity rather than debating whether we "*are* calm."
e. There is no surer sign that someone wants to be heard than raising their voice. Relatedly, there is also no more certain signal that they feel that they are *not* being heard. Usually, once they understand that they are being listened to, they will adjust their own volume independently, without having to be told to do so.

32

The key to constructive resolution is focusing on solutions versus problems. This requires acknowledging feelings and shifting away from past misfortune to what is possible in the future.

33

Our energy is best used attending to feelings versus facts. Do *not* respond with logic and explanations but with emotional understanding.

Agree with their feeling rather than debating accuracy. If you are disputing, cease.

Factual legitimacy is far from a shield. You can be right and still get your ass kicked. It happens to people every single day.

a. Emotions are the area of agreement. No matter how wrongheaded the person's position or conduct, they feel what they feel regardless of whether we think they "should."

b. All behavior is communication and asks a question. Fundamentally that question is: will this conduct "work" by being rewarded? The acting out individual is raising a query which fundamentally translates to "Can I get away with this?"

c. Arguing doesn't change people's minds but instead most often cements their position. We cannot win the arguments of whether we are prejudicial toward someone, like them or want to help. It's more beneficial to acknowledge how horrible it must feel to believe that those things are occurring.

d. The correctness of our facts usually only further

entrenches the polarity of right/wrong, as opposed to helping find commonality.

e. A recurring error people make is attempting to use math to counter people's emotions. This leads to devastating faux pas such as "Well, at least you still have two other children" or inquiring how old an elder was when they passed, as if age lessens the impact.

These attempts at "reason" are catastrophic since emotions are not calculable and addressing them as if they are only boosts the recipient's sense of desolation. Rather than consoling, these incidents confirm that others do not understand the level of suffering, no matter how much they might profess to.

34

Specificity equals credibility. Any precise estimate is more likely believed than "all" or "none," "never" and "always."

Being specific also helps free us from the quicksand of our own subjectivity and exaggeration.

35

All forms of abusive relationships and addictive cycles share the same pattern: the trap of the victim attempting to rationalize about the irrational process from which the other party is operating.

a. The actor *does* "know better," but they're driven to enact the poorly advised behavior anyway.
b. Interpersonally, focusing on exceptions hijacks our empathy and creates the circularly abusive hazard— the conflation of he "*can* be sweet" with someone actually dependably "being kind."

36

For far too many relationships, betrayal serves as a substitute for intimacy due to the unhealthy intensity that follows.

a. There is a natural terror of intimacy and the vulnerability that it requires. Therefore, most relationships end due to self-sabotage right at the exact moment that they are truly beginning—on the threshold of full, voluntary submission to the possibility of being hurt. Exactly then is when most of us panic and flee.

37

Intentions do not equal outcomes.

a.   Those who defend actions based on their intents are behaving puritanically and fear that any imperfection contaminates and makes them "bad," rather than providing a learning opportunity that can help them grow.

38

"Just say no," to yes/no questions. They define the world in an overly simplistic way and force individuals to prematurely commit to all-or-nothing positions rather than landing more softly and realistically along the continuum.

Yes/no structures are actually statements masquerading as questions and imply that there is a right-or-wrong answer.

These types of questions inflame anxiety, for no one wants to be incorrect and "fail." The odds of receiving either a yes or no reply are fundamentally 50/50—the same odds as chance. Therefore, these questions do not increase our likelihood of success in persuasion. In fact, they often make it worse. Negatively inclined individuals tend to reply "no" more often than not, while those that tend toward positivity often answer "yes" even when in doubt.

And once someone has committed to a no, it's highly improbable that they'll reverse their position, as people strive toward consistency in their decisions.

Further, if right-or-wrong is introduced or indicated, it's a rare individual that's not convinced that they are the righteous one.

a. Instead, utilize "What" and "How" questions that require more care, thought, and nuance than black-and-white constructions. "What" and "How" solicit information rather than judgment.

b. These open "How" and "What" questions tend to elicit more honest and detailed information, whereas closed, yes/no questions often coerce.

Not "Is everything all right?" but "*How* are you feeling?"

c. "Yes/no" questions can often be avoided by instead focusing exclusively and matter-of-factly on the outcome that is desired. For example, "We'd like to sit there," versus the excessively deferential, "Would it be okay if I sit there?"

d. Avoid metacommunications. This is where many yes/no questions reside. Do not talk about talking. Doing so is the opposite of using hypnotic language since explicit references to the communication itself trigger hyperconsciousness of what's being discussed.

Instead, simply speak.

Not "Do you want to talk about it?" but "What's going on?" Avoid "Is it okay if I ask you a question?" in favor of "How are you feeling?

39

The more constructive focal point is not on "If," but "How" a crisis will be resolved. The existence of solutions in some form must not be doubted but instead foregrounded.

a. After identifying some awareness of what the other party is feeling, we should quickly shift to offering alternative options—"Unfortunately, that is not possible, but *this* is."

40

Communication is not a rigid boiler-plate. It is best tailored to the relational framework at hand.

Is it a social, asocial, or antisocial encounter? Each must be managed differently. Trying to be "nice" with an antisocial actor will almost invariably backfire, since it's misfit for the occasion. This is a common error of people with good intentions who are in denial of the circumstantial parameters that they are currently facing.

a. Aside from individuals who know or love us, discussions should customarily center on "What" is happening rather than "Who" it is happening to, for "Who" is *not* the basis of the relationship. We have been thrown together involuntarily with another party due to a *potentially* shared purpose (e.g., serving a random customer at a store).

   We can accomplish this shift in focus by using the impersonal pronouns of "what/that/it/this" versus the divisive "I/you" and "yes/no" formations that most social communication utilizes.

   During asocial encounters, there is a triangulation present rather than the two-way ricochet of social interactions. Our emphasis can be placed on that third element—the reason we are interacting versus the participants.

   "It is not about *you* (or me); it's about *that*."

41

Primary words of imprisonment are: can't, have, should.

a. Absolute language imprisons us by denying choice any time we are faced with the imperfection of the universe.

b. Extreme language communicates someone's emotional state, not the factual reality. And thereby, it also incites argument and debate. Additionally, it undermines the credibility of the speaker due to their words' inaccuracy.

c. This is a common trap in intimate relationships. The aroused partner overstates their position, then the other debates the merits of those words rather than conceding the intensity of feeling that is being conveyed.

d. When people speak of what isn't possible, most commonly they are referring to things that are difficult, though not truly impossible (e.g., "I can't quit my job."). This results in inertia and an increased sense of powerlessness that ratchets the tension more.

e. Aside from the clinically identified sadistic (who thankfully make up less than 1 percent of the general population), most assailants feel that they're the victim. And it is true: they *are* victims—of their own narrow and rigid ideology and the language which straitjackets them, making the external world their despot.

f.   Much human folly arises from either the obstinance of what one feels that they "can't" do or misguided actions undertaken based on "having" to do something, even when it's inadvisable to do so.

g.   To soften our thinking, practice holding two seemingly contradictory thoughts at once (e.g., "Yes, they can often be a notably exhausting person, but they also possess passion and integrity when it comes to working with children at risk"). This is what nonabsolute, specific words help us do—to see the world in color versus black-and-white. To let the gray in.

h.   Rather than extreme language being used beneficially to personally forbid specific acts, it's instead regrettably most often used to except and justify these actions under certain conditions. The only use of such language that tends to be constructive is when vowing internally to never commit odious, off-limits behaviors (e.g., "No matter *how* angry my child makes me, I will never hit them, period"), rather than retaining permission for exceptions that are very likely to someday occur.

42

Among the words of liberation are: might/may, some, one, can, almost, seems.

a. "Might" is the mightiest of the antidepressant/antiargument words, as it allows for all possibility. No matter how rare, unlikely, or lopsided the case, something *might* still be true or possible on *occasion*.

b. "Some" is the most accurate sum. Some people, some of the time versus everyone, *all* the time.

c. "Almost" keeps the factual door ajar rather than slamming it shut. There is a world of difference between *almost* always and always, *almost* never and never.

d. The way something "seems" is quite different than what it "is" or how they "are."

e. Our energy is more productively utilized concentrating on what can or could be, rather than what we "can't" do.

f. Use of these precise words increases the validity of our statements, elevates subtlety over brute force, and tethers us more closely to reality.

43

In order for any communication to be successful, three hurdles must be crossed:

- Hearing the message.
- Understanding the message.
- Believing that the information being conveyed is true.

The third factor is what's most often overlooked. Dismayingly, people are frequently injured by someone who has actually issued an explicit warning that was not attended to, but dismissed.

Critical to our own credibility are behavioral regularity combined with factual accuracy.

44

To be truly nonjudgmental, it is necessary to describe specific actions versus imposing labels. Someone is "behaving badly," rather than *is* a "bad person."

a. I am not a bad person. I am not a good person. I am a person who has done both bad and good things in different proportions under different circumstances.

And my having never reached certain extremities of depravity (e.g., murder) does not exempt me from my lapses in conduct.

b. Beware of statements that start with "I'm the kind of person who . . ." for that individual is defining themselves as a monolith rather than an elaborate blend.

c. We should be leery of anything that's claimed as 100 percent. Like sentences starting with, "There are two types of people in the world . . ."

d. Labelling people, neighborhoods, or nations as "violent" actually enacts violence. For doing so denies nuance and goodness.

Calling someone an angry person is itself an angry action.

e. *You* are not bad, but sometimes what you've done is less than flawless.

And that is okay.

In fact, it is normal. And we remain valuable regardless.

45

In asocial or antisocial encounters, personal pronouns should be avoided almost entirely since the people involved are not the primary basis for the relationship as is the case in a social encounter. We didn't choose them (e.g., the passenger next to us on an airplane), and they didn't choose us, but we are working together currently to try to meet a specific goal or goals.

a. In reality, it is rarely about me or you but rather "us" and "what."

b. If pronouns are used at all, communicational influence is largely dependent on the use of pronoun accenting. Where or on whom we place the emphasis when speaking can act as a volume knob—dramatically arousing or lessening emotional impact. For example, "*I* was wondering what your thoughts are," is far different from, "I want to know *your* thoughts." Even better is an absence of personal pronouns: "*What* feedback is there?"

These emphases are where people's unconscious bias or passive aggression often oozes out.

c. Sadly, many people's personal reference index is sky-high. They struggle to communicate anything without reference to self or even *multiple* references to themselves in a single sentence.

46

Intentional and careful communication is advisable. Though this thoughtfulness requires a more methodical investment of effort, it actually saves us energy in the long run by preventing crises from manifesting as often.

a. "Careful communication" equals the use of measured messages. That is our pinpointing precise descriptions versus blanket claims of value. Rather than ever allegedly being the "best," we can speak about how I've been active as a lecturer for more than thirty years and have never missed a single class. Whether I'm any "good" remains highly debatable, but what's been stated instead is objective and verifiable.

b. Counterintuitively, people that speak a second or third (or fourth or more) language often excel in crisis situations versus those who might be more fluent, but then tend to put their foot in their mouth by responding too quickly. If one is not entirely confident about an ability to communicate, we tend to work harder to prevent being misunderstood.

c. If we spoke routinely with the same care as on first dates or at a job interview, we'd rarely find ourselves in error.

47

Dialogue management is based on two chief techniques. Both involve active and goal-directed processes rather than casual ones.

a. Mirror questions: the answering of questions with questions. Often the question to be asked is the same one that's been asked of us.

   In short, change the subject. Don't allow yourself to become the focus, unless that is your choice.

b. Broken-record responses: continue firmly but gently stating the truth until the other party first hears it, and then ultimately begins to accept. This is not a robotic action. Nonetheless, our answer need not change. The person generally just needs time to adjust.

   It is important in doing this that we don't let our message become muddied by negative tone.

48

There are two main pivot words that help temper exchanges. Both should be used liberally.

a. "Unfortunately" is a most fortunate word. Making the effort to verbalize these five mere syllables can determine all the difference in how a message is received. The word demonstrates to some degree our understanding of the other's position—without overtly claiming to—while also prepping them for the rejection and disappointment that they are facing.
b. Use of "okay" is not factual agreement but merely acknowledgement that we've heard them and that they believe whatever they believe, right or wrong.

49

A magic question during conflict is, "What do you think would be the best possible solution?"

This places the responsibility on the individual and guides them to think more constructively. Even if their desired solution proves not available, this question still softens the stiffness of their position and allows for the possible consideration of alternative options.

50

There is much peril in embedded commands. Therefore, be careful not to structure messages negatively but instead use positive and unambiguous terms—to speak of what we want versus what we do *not* want.

a. When we verbalize what we don't want, we continue to advertise the very thing we ostensibly are trying to abolish. The dictate "Don't think about _____," still requires the person to consider that which they are told to negate. Thus, the identified problem remains the focus.

   Rather than telling a group of schoolchildren, "Don't run," the clearer direction is "Slow down."

   "Stop panicking!" is likely to be met with nothing but.

51

Limit-setting best exists as a form of information-giving, not punishment. The key question is whether an intervention can have any constructive, future benefit or simply constitutes a mean-spirited, after-the-fact shaming.

a. Unhealthy behavior is unstable: it worsens if continued. That is, conduct escalates until a fitting consequence results—an accident, injury, illness, punishment. Any indiscretion left unchecked is rewarded. Nourished, it grows. We do no one any favors by allowing such actions to repetitively go unchecked. This is how tyrants are spawned.

b. You can't "spoil" a kid with love, only hate. When I've been undesirably placed in a position to set limits with my daughter's friends who are acting out, what strikes me is that rather than resentment, their response is one of gladness and even muted joy.

　　Yesterday, my heart was wrenched when a neighbor confided how their mother had hit them for "no reason." There could never be a reason good enough to do so.

52

In imminently dangerous situations—such as someone who is about to step unwittingly in front of an oncoming bus—all communication is better contracted to single syllables and repetition.

a. The key words to interrupt a person's negative physical motion are "don't," "stop," "now," and their name (if known). These words should be repeated loudly and clearly until hopefully some pause is given. These utterances also help attract help more reliably than shouting for it.

   While someone is stomping another person on the ground is not the time to process the assailant's challenging childhood.

b. If you are the one in danger, these same words, repetition, and vocal volume should be used. But, if neutral bystanders are present, attempt also to appeal directly to individuals and with specific tasks (e.g., "Sir, please dial 911 now.").

   Due to social proof theory, we are, paradoxically, less likely to get help when there are *more* people around since the sense of responsibility is dispersed and the inaction of others copied contagiously. Conversely, a lone person often times feels compelled to act, as the full burden is theirs and there is no status quo to conform to.

53

Crisis is usually due to a failure of curiosity—an unwilling-ness to explore the entire spectrum and engage with the nonbinary intricacy of human dynamics.

a.   Ordinarily, it is advisable to listen before speaking, and to ask questions before making statements.

54

To provide constructive context and proportion, attempt to state something positive about the circumstance before offering any negative feedback to other parties. Investing that minimal effort to say something good before saying something "bad" tends to have outsized impact.

a. Contrastingly, stating anything negative at the start will reflexively trigger another person's defensiveness and almost always shut down listening and receptivity.
b. This "Yes, first" practice also impels us to seek out more balance and complexity regarding the issues faced.

55

It is prudent to search for the secondary gains that result from a seemingly self-destructive behavior or act (e.g., a child being rewarded with energy whenever they act out).

a. Fundamentally, most often what individuals are seeking is attention, no matter what the costs.
b. Do not take goodness for granted. Too often the best-behaved are neglected in favor of the "trouble-makers." It doesn't take long for the ignored to identify what course need be taken to receive attention.

56

Emotionally, people are usually only changed lastingly by processes, not events. After a major trauma or windfall, there naturally is a corresponding response. But over time, most individuals drift back toward their baseline. If they were depressed before winning the lottery, the depression will again return. If they were generally a happy-go-lucky type, that will gradually reassert itself in a modified form.

a. Beware that almost everyone becomes a better and more contemplative person during the lull following a crisis. The task is to find a way to sustain that sensitivity and gratitude over days, weeks, years, or across a lifetime. Doing so requires consistent effort—ensuring that we have not just been acted upon by an incident but are consciously and habitually taking new, purposeful, and repeated strides toward betterment.

57

Regret plays a massive role in recovery. Whenever any potential solutions have been missed, the ability to accept the ultimate outcome is detrimentally impacted. Thus, prevention possesses even greater value beyond just the moment at hand.

58

Humans (and most other creatures) are loss-aversive—routinely we are more motivated by what we can lose than gain. Regret avoidance drives decision-making. Thus, the paralysis of the "what ifs."

Conservatism is driven by the dread of change being stronger than the discomfort with the current circumstances—the fearfulness that things could get worse from that which is at least "familiar" and hasn't killed us . . . *yet*.

a. It's almost never advisable to tell people what they could've had, because anything other than that will never measure up to their imagination of what could've been. Instead, it is advisable to spotlight whatever is currently available and possible.

b. It is prudent to *under*promise rather than overpromise. This remains so even in the cases where outcomes are positive but nonetheless were less than what was expected or predicted. It's better for another party to be pleasantly surprised than disappointed.

   Far more desirable is that any benefits reaped are seen as bonuses rather than having fallen short somehow.

c. Zero is not a neutral number, nor simple math. The difference between one and zero is not merely one but immeasurable. The emotional response to this difference is not rational. That is why if we cost someone *any* pain, symbolically the impact is the same regardless of the amount.

d. Thus, most people will work harder for free—if they have volunteered to—than for money. But once a dollar figure is introduced, judgment immediately sets in as to whether any compensation is good enough.

The inversion of the zero principle is that others will often treat us like crap when they are not paying us anything because psychologically they feel that they don't have anything to lose since nothing has been invested and no value given. Paradoxically, if they are *overpaying* someone, their reverence toward the employed often becomes a self-fulfilling prophecy. Almost nobody wants to have been "wrong" about an investment and to experience the regret that results.

59

The economics of emotion result in human energy being largely nonmathematical. Some emotions provide energy, while others take and drain. Most people function at an energetic deficit much of the time.

a. Commonly, we face grave difficulty embarking on undertakings that seem too immense or daunting. The trick is to start somewhere, *anywhere*, and build momentum.

60

Paradoxically, we often reserve our greatest enmity for those most like us—the threateningly similar others. Until we make peace with those most akin, authentic acceptance of all others remains elusive.

a. Instead, intimacy and empathy are often displaced to safer and less intimidating subjects—those who we actually care about *little*. The most common issue for many is rarely an utter absence or lack of compassion on the part of that person but rather their diverting care to less-fitting recipients.
b. There is nothing one can hate quite as intensely as oneself.

61

Your family isn't necessarily "so fucked up." You just know them better than others due to having been forced to confront their flaws. This is unlike our experience with most strangers or acquaintances who we do not fully know well at all.

a. I'm horrified anytime someone I've just met claims how much they like me or that I am "great." Clearly, they don't know me very well and are undoubtedly bound for disappointment once they do.

62

Comparisons tend to be violent. Avoidance of comparisons allows us to be more specific about each individual person and circumstance, rather than judgmental. For example, "She's the best player" and "They are better than you" are vastly different from the precision of "He is the second-highest scorer in the history of the school." The latter stands on its own and is nondebatable. It is fact-based rather than editorial.

a. Akin to this, any loss which is more ambiguous and less defined is harder to garner support and understanding from others for, and thus tends to lead to deeper isolation. In this way, obvious and "larger" tragedy is often more easily metabolized than that which is fainter and disguised, though potentially just as damaging.

63

Instant re-prioritization is the goal in crisis.

a. What mattered and was the focus seconds before (e.g.,
    preservation of material items like clothing, grocer-
    ies, or smartphones; or being in a "rush" for time),
    abruptly becomes virtually inconsequential.

    Many injuries result from attempts to have it both
    ways, so to speak. Wanting to walk away with zero
    consequences—without having spilled even a drop
    of a take-away cappuccino—rather than making clear
    and swift decisions about what's valued most. With
    bleak frequency, people throw away everything in
    attempts to stave off even the most trivial concession.

b. In a crisis, those seconds or minutes are the bridge to
    the rest of our life. Far too many flounder making that
    crossing due to their freezing up or the reluctance to
    move forward constructively.

    Though uninvited, these junctures are among the
    most vital in our existence.

c. What we are trying to develop is "instant hindsight"—
    to shake the shock of a sudden crisis posthaste and
    fully address the options related to the reality now
    faced, however unpleasant or ominous it may be.

d. With my young daughter, I've had to quell the
    tendency when I'm busy to see her attempts to
    connect as "interruptions" and instead realize that

what I think is "important" in that moment is rarely even remotely the more invaluable thing.

I repeatedly remind myself that soon I will pine for her attentions after she will have moved on in her life and no longer have such desire or interest. Thus, I force myself to stop and treasure these opportunities. Exact moments like these have occurred countless times while writing this very book, instances when I tear myself away from laptop myopia to take in the bigger picture of where the real work is to be done.

e. Much damage results from failures of imagination—either by not envisioning ramifications or by fantasizing that results will be horrendously different than those that are likely to occur (e.g., almost no one believes beforehand that they're going to be hurt or die from a choice. Otherwise, they would almost never have taken that same path).

f. An aspect of this is that people often deepen crisis due to politeness and concern with appearances.

Once, I was at a taquería and a woman who was choking quietly stood and moved into a corner so as not to disturb anyone. She was pre-inclined to expire discreetly rather than cause any disturbance to other diners. (Fortunately, the years of annual Heimlich maneuver classes that hospital employees are required to take finally proved their worth.)

g. Individuals who routinely make poor choices colonize the life of those closest to them—it is their partner who will nurse them in a coma after a motorcycle accident; their young son is the one who'll be all but orphaned when their parent is incarcerated for assaulting a stranger.

h. And though it is best to minimize unnecessary risk, we should also shun gutless caution if faced with the opportunity to potentially prevent greater injury or crisis.

64

A much overlooked folly of anger is that it produces dishonesty. Whenever the revelation of our feelings is met with protest, we tend to shut down and stop sharing the truth entirely, particularly with those who've been critical.

a. This is harmful since emotions are our guidance system, an interpersonal GPS. When feelings are denied, we eventually end up stranded on a precipice without even having realized how lost we'd become.
b. Secrets make us sick. Harboring secrets is like acting as an accomplice to a fugitive. It provides refuge for the "criminal" elements within ourselves.

65

"Entertaining the absurd" is a primary remedy to depression.

a. If we allow ourselves to stretch and deliberately consider the most ridiculous scenarios we can envision, then in comparison almost any solution along the spectrum suddenly becomes more admissible as a possibility.

b. Retain doubt. Leave the side door cracked for uncertainty.

66

Lawlessness frequently results from the gap between formal and informal law—life as written, not lived.

a. Organic agreement among the majority in a community is necessary for self-sustaining peace—the rules must attune with what people feel to be true rather than obedience being enforced from on high. Else, citizens resent the daily reality that they're met with and must therefore be externally coerced and policed.

b. The only thing worse than a needed limit not being set is a limit being set and not enforced. The latter rewards defiance, empties words of meaning, undermines credibility, and weakens authority.

   Don't ever set a restriction unless you're willing to back it up straightaway *and* recurrently.

c. The healthiest society has fewer laws but consistent enforcement of whatever laws exist.

67

Double binds marks a pinnacle of machination and trickery—the placing of someone else in a position where they are damned no matter which choice they make and, thus, become immobilized by that conundrum.

The objective of double binds is sheer control at any costs. Those who do not command sturdy self-control are driven to control others and the environment, which ironically often ultimately results in control being denied or imposed on them (e.g., prison).

This parental style corresponds most highly to the development of psychosis in offspring since we can often orient ourselves to extreme environments (e.g., knowing what to expect), but inconsistency is extremely difficult to adapt to.

If one can't ever do anything "right," we usually cease trying at all.

68

Almost any violence is "senseless" (with the exception of last resort self-defense or defense of others). Use of the term itself is a redundancy.

a. Relatedly, all rape is a hate crime.
b. And it is a fairy tale that we can "win" a fight or war. Something has already been lost if any damaging conflict has emerged.

69

The question should not be, "What emotion are you experiencing right now?," but plural: "Which *emotions*?"

a. Emotions arise in blends (e.g., when a loved one passes away we are not *just* sad, as is societally prescribed and expected. Often, we also experience relief, guilt, anger, or other feelings, to varying degrees).
b. Almost nothing arises from a single source but a confluence of factors.
c. Though things usually did not originate from *only* "that," they did not *not* arise from it, either. What's cited plausibly did play a part, however miniscule.

    The claim "I didn't do anything" states an impossibility. The person did *something* regardless of whether there was culpability.

    When someone criticizes another by hurling an absolutist label like, "You're a complete shithead," that extravagant statement nonetheless could bear some grain of truth. Rather than defending against the distorted nature of the claim, it's still possible to grant that, "Yes, it is true that my behavior was less than irreproachable."

    Willingness to admit some fault tends to go far further—particularly with people that we don't know well—than the stock apology of "I'm sorry," which inordinately fixates on us and our experience.

d. An inclination to believe certain things that may largely be unpopular does not by itself constitute open-mindedness but can instead simply attest to a classic case of contrarianism. True open-mindedness is the commitment to potentially embrace ideas that we find highly disagreeable and that run counter to our existing beliefs—a willingness to be "wrong."

70

All successful interventions share one basic principle: breaking the existing pattern.

a. The answer to, "What should you do when _____ happens?" is "*Lots* of different things. As many as possible (... if you're fortunate enough to even have the chance)."
b. There is no singular solution. Flexibility is the antidote to rigidity. Experiment and utilize intuition until some action hopefully induces a disruption in the negative cycle, even if that intervention is something that would not commonly be prescribed.
c. Paradoxically, often the solution is to do exactly the opposite of what we've done previously (e.g., silence versus speaking, accepting rather than directing, and so on).

    In general, if you're late or hurried, slow down.
d. Sometimes the most caring thing you can do for someone is give them a smackdown (metaphorically speaking), that is if gentler means have proven inadequate.
e. The range of possibility should always include not doing or saying anything at all.
f. There is only one thing that works all the time: nothing.
g. Another example: With lip-reading for the deaf, experts advise that rather than speaking louder or more

slowly—as people often do when the recipient is having trouble understanding what is being said—one should instead try rephrasing the message entirely.

71

Practice surrender—letting go of the control that we never even had.

72

It is advisable to strive for balance physically in the environment as well as emotionally.

a. Stand when they stand, sit if they sit.
b. Position ourselves *beside* versus against them, to become aligned and also allow them a path forward to flee, should they desire.
c. Ensure that the gap between us is never too far or too close. Generally, that sweet spot is approximately just beyond *their* arm's reach.

73

Paradoxically, the more meaningful an action, the less conscious an actor often is of it.

a. Words themselves are most likely to lie since their purpose is to explicitly "tell" something.
b. Bodily, the feet tend to be the most honest—where energy leaks more (e.g., a tapping foot) due to their being furthest from the head.
c. Something may not be "on my mind" but still linger on my subconscious. This is another reason why regular emotional self-audits are paramount.

74

An overarching goal is to tolerate the gray areas and strive to live along the continuum, amid the spectrum—fighting the urge for false certainty and spurning the counterfeit comfort that dichotomies and rigidity provide.

a. The correct answer to most either/or equations is, "Both (. . . to *some* degree)." Or in a few exceptionally negative cases, the suitable response may instead be "neither."

Proportions and percentages, not zero-sum calculations reflect reality more robustly.

b. As long as someone is ambivalent about undertaking a negative action, hope endures.

Someone telling me that they are going to kick my ass is a gift. Though it is not what I'd most like to hear, it serves as an explicit warning and indicates that they remain undecided about the course of action.

For ourselves, ambivalence can provide a warning sign that self-inventory is urgently needed to get to the heart of our feelings. A common phenomenon is people not realizing that they were angry (or how angry they were) until undertaking a violent action. After-the-fact is much too late to discover what we're feeling.

As with anger, ambivalence is a secondary state—cultivated by a reluctance to explore or face the more primal emotions bubbling below.

c. Proportions must perpetually be kept in view. A false equivalency in narratives is commonly generated when people say, "Let's hear from the other side." It's actually very often not "the other side" but the other *extreme* that is being given equal time, even though they usually represent only a sliver of general opinion and sentiment.

d. If we personally abolished the use of the absolute words (e.g., "am," "are," "is," et cetera) as well as *un*-nuanced proclamations when speaking of people and events, the world would become a much more peaceful place. The objective is to communicate the specifics of what is happening rather than casting judgements or assigning permanent labels.

e. There are no entirely "disabled people." People's abilities are often just concentrated in other areas, ones generally invisible to the dominant society.

Who truly are the disabled ones? For even the sighted and hearing among us remain deaf and blind to most of our surroundings.

75

The pyramid of psychological defense mechanisms are: denial, projection, and reaction-formations.

a. Whenever denial falters, blame is projected—usually through the use of the word "you."
b. Reaction-formations claim the exact opposite emotion(s) of what's actually felt. Through this, a person unintentionally reveals how much they must actually care to "hate" someone or something.
c. The human tendency toward reaction-formations means that whenever we do choose to assist someone, it is best for *our own* well-being that we do so unconditionally, since those that we help will often viscerally resent us for our assistance no matter how illogical and contradictory that is.

76

Sadly, the most common way of coping with scary events is blaming the victim. This projection allows others to forge distance, and restore the illusion that the world makes sense and that tragedies only happen to those who "deserve" it. Regarding an individual who has been victimized as being at fault inappropriately designates them as different than us. This allows us to thereby continue to falsely assume that we possess immunity to such threats.

77

No matter what the topic, people most often are talking about themselves.

a. What they see in others is frequently a reflection of their own person. It is so much easier to recognize the faults in others that we deny in ourselves, for those follies are so very familiar.

b. Further, that which a person rejects in themselves is often their *most* prevalent trait. Anyone who declares that they are "not a liar" has just lied by making that claim, since no one is entirely truthful about everything. One of my considerable stumbles in life was being a people-pleaser. I remained factually spot-on though regrettably often not emotionally honest. It's tough to tell the truth when you've yet to reconcile with it.

The person who ignores our bad breath is "acting nice," while the one who politely points out that we have spinach in our teeth is actually *being* nice. Though their candor is unlikely to usher forth stunning popularity, they're concretely enacting kindness rather than merely miming an empty performance of it.

78

A ruling factor in personal conduct is energy conservation. Fundamentally, we are lazy and resistant to doing most anything that we don't *have* to do. This results in our often gambling with negative outcomes or tragedy—the playing of odds and childish hope that nothing bad results from a potentially foreseeable conundrum.

79

Ultimately, it is the net effect of any action that must be weighed. Is the solution sustainable? Both extremes—either being too harsh or too lenient—can create the illusion of ending conflict but actually postpone and ultimately aggravate it.

Whenever people claim that their variant, imbalanced approach "works," it's usually others who pay the price for such deviations (e.g., those who then set reasonable limits will consequently be met with the even greater resistance that results from an improper precedent that their pacifying peer has set—the other parent, a fellow teacher, et al.—to curry favor and carve out a sense of exceptionalism).

a.   Instead, confronting and enduring a short-term clash might result in longer-term health interpersonally. In fact, successfully weathering an emotional storm with another party is one of the more bonding experiences individuals can share.

80

Trauma tends to arrive delayed, cyclically, and in a nonlinear fashion.

a. Due to shock, a person paradoxically often appears "better" immediately following a tragic event than they will months, years or decades down the line.
b. Our society sells us on the hocus-pocus of epiphanies. In fact, our recovery from trauma is usually not instantaneous but ongoing, irregular, and a lifetime project.

81

To concretely enact empathy requires striving toward other-centeredness—active attempts to understand experiences and perspectives radically different from our own.

a. The larger test is not whether we can provide love and support to someone we like but whether we can do so with individuals toward whom we feel unsympathetic or less empathic.

   The higher achievement is to do the more noble thing not just when it comes easily but also when it requires Herculean effort.

82

For lasting coexistence to occur, the needed emphasis is working from the viewpoint of cooperation versus competition.

a. Too often, capitalistic societies promote the fiction of competition and noncollectivity. Yet, we are all dependent on others for survival, and most of those people that have helped will remain unknown to us or even are long deceased (e.g., the laborers who built the subway system we depend on daily for travel are anonymous to virtually every rider).

b. Win/Win outlooks promote hopefulness, while Win/Lose models inherently provoke anxiety.

83

Anger and hydraulics are intrinsically linked. Actions that seem to come out of the blue have instead usually been building over time until they reached a breaking point.

a. No matter how unpleasant or unsettling the process, it is much better for someone to reveal their truest feelings or urges, rather than conceal them. A warning or threat is always a cry for help also, no matter how strained or strangled.

b. When it's claimed that there was no warning, what's really meant is that there was no *explicit* warning. Yes, maybe the individual did not sent us a detailed memo weeks in advance. Nonetheless, there were almost always signs that could've been heeded.

Just because someone didn't say it doesn't mean it wasn't shown.

84

Any time a figure behaves differently for an audience than otherwise, an ethical alarm is raised. True integrity is behaving the same whether one is being watched or not watched, rewarded, or penalized.

a. A person being "nice" far from guarantees that they *are* nice. The key is consistency. Often, a seemingly gruff individual possesses far deeper decency than a friendly one.

b. A person's or a society's integrity can be judged quite well by how they treat those over whom they hold greater power.

c. Since character is based on constancy, if we are ever going to take on anybody, we'd better be willing to confront *everyone*—not just those ostensibly smaller and weaker than us.

d. If we witness without protest the mistreatment of a marginalized person or group, we are not exempt. We are *next*.

e. Inequality itself is an act of violence.

85

Characterological individuals are claim-stakers. They're hunting for real estate inside another's brain. The more that we find ourselves consumed by distressful thoughts about a person, the more aggressive the disease.

These persistently, personality-disordered individuals work to get us to assume the doubt and reflection that they are unwilling or unable to engage in. Thereby, we're tricked into undertaking that emotional labor on their behalf.

86

When we are assessing others, there are two universal factors we need examine:

a. Extremes in behavior—both the obvious and its other half, the more subterranean actions.
b. Changes in behavior (e.g., weight loss/gain). Even a change seemingly for the better might indicate something otherwise. A typically mean person suddenly becoming affable, for instance, could actually veil trouble.

    No one element in isolation always indicates the identical thing. Yes, someone might cross their arms because they're feeling defensive, but it could also merely mean that they're cold or experiencing back pain.

    Do not allow the novel to pass without closer examination. If every person in a crowd is wearing shorts and tank tops except for one in a wool trench coat, gloves, and stocking cap, that demands a second look. If your partner makes a remark or reference that they've never before, that is worth exploring.

    Danger generally presents itself any time there is a transition, even ones that are apparently more favorable. Try to regularly assess the familiar with new eyes, as if seeing them or it for the first time.

87

The myth of social equity is that our past good deeds increase our odds for future success. But with strangers, we are always starting from scratch. No matter how charitable we've been in our lifetime, that individual is unaware of this and evaluates us based exclusively on the evidence that they see before them (along with the prejudices that they bring to this exchange). Each encounter is isolated and begins from zero or even a deficit. We carry over no surplus or goodwill from prior instances.

a. Belief in past performance influencing our current dynamic is largely tied to the hollow hope that the world is fair, makes sense, and that people receive what they deserve versus the harsher reality that our benevolent deeds must be undertaken for their own intrinsic rewards.

b. Relatedly, many treat love as finite. Paradoxically, they also tend to squander their miserliness with strangers instead of lavishing it on those who actually love or care for them. These are the people who often instead are mistreated because their devotion is seen as a given and disregarded complacently.

88

The starvation for solutions and closure rushes people into seeking easy answers and fixes.

a. Too often myopic, short-term concerns interfere with long-term goals. This presents a mix-up in priorities whereby the tiniest elements interfere with the big picture. For example, someone hesitating to cancel a wedding because the invitations have already been sent and huge amounts of money spent. This trepidation may be understandable but incalculably costlier down the line.

b. Similarly, all addictions share that though they might provide immediate gratification they prove more expensive and devastating in the end.

89

Past behavior is statistically the foremost indicator of future behavior. Nonetheless, if assessing the likelihood that an action will be repeated, three factors are crucial to consider.

a. Repetition: how many times has a person taken this action? The behavioral algebra is complex. Having done something twice rather than once is not doubly significant but astronomically more telling—it all but eliminates that the first occurrence was an isolated or unlucky case.

b. Recentness: almost all of us have done some inadvisable or "crazy" things when we are young. But if we're fortunate enough to survive those instances, they usually become compartmentalized within our youth and are not repeated in adulthood.

    Most violent actions wane as people age, dropping sharply during one's early to midtwenties, and falling off almost entirely in our midforties. (That is, until there is an upswing toward the end of life when some people experience cognitive reductions, which are often coupled with a sense of hopelessness and/ or the surfacing of resentments and regret.)

    More than whether someone has done something, *when* they did it tends to be the most relevant feature.

c. Intensity and escalation: how severe was the action? And is it stable or getting worse?

90

Due to the repetition-compulsion, we generally tend to repeat most behaviors, no matter how destructive they are. We are largely creatures of habit. This helps us automate our daily conduct which then frees up more room for newly emerging problems.

Even conflict and agony can grow familiar, almost comforting—a home base by default, mistaken as normal should we become acclimated to them.

a. Therefore, be mindful that any first step in the wrong direction is knotty and troublesome to undo. The easiest way to prevent catastrophe is not to toy with it in the first place.

b. The common belief is that people will become much like their parents or other role models. Though occurring more rarely, the opposite can also be the case. Exposure to negative examples can serve as a graphic road map of what to adamantly avoid (e.g., the child of an alcoholic being a teetotaler).

91

Active observation requires rhythmically searching for cues and clues, particularly seeking out subtler actions for any buried and masked meaning.

a. Active observation stands opposite of denial, and instead engages in recognition and acceptance of uncomfortable truths. In these cases, we are "looking for trouble," not to engage with but quell.

b. Systematically search from the outset for the unfore-seen use of any new technology or solution—the by-product(s). Our survival instinct guarantees people's ingenuity in finding ways to get their needs met with whatever tools are at one's disposal, no matter what their designed purpose.

c. Cause-and-effect should not be concealed by the novelty and convenience that something new presents. Rather than waiting to see what happens, we should seek clear vision before even jumping in.

92

Interpersonal trade deficits are telling.

a. Be alert to those who speak more about themselves than others, who enact soliloquies rather inquiry.
b. Additionally, these are generally individuals who, though they behave insensitively to others (and often even claim that they are "an empath"), are exceptionally fragile to any perceived injury toward themselves.
c. Particularly telling are people who feel that they're entitled to privileges that others are not.
d. And the most chilling combination in terms of violent outbursts are those with an enlarged sense of self-worth coupled with a dearth of real world success. This formula evokes constant disappointment and disillusion.

93

A telltale, concerning flag is that certain behaviors come clustered with other larger behaviors, rather than happening in isolation (e.g., the person who chooses to adopt a statistically ultra-aggressive dog, signals further entitlement and extraordinariness by leaving said dog off leash).

a. When bright lines are crossed that most other people do not ever trespass (e.g., torture), those actions routinely serve as behavioral DNA: one small sample well represents the whole.
b. It is advisable to differentiate between situational outbursts versus ongoing patterns. Most people in crisis will return to more "normal" and baseline behaviors once a situation is resolved, and may even express remorse or regret for their previous, out of the ordinary actions.

   In contrast, those with consistent characterological issues will simply move on to a new complaint or demand, and even an escalated one. Ongoing attempts to help them only lead to increased sickness.

94

The more disproportionate someone's reaction is, the more likely it is based on factors that are invisible to us. Most pain is referential, the roots tangled and far removed.

a. Though we might be the current, easily accessible target, very little that happens on the planet—both good and bad—has anything to do with us.

95

Crisis usually occurs wherever there is convergence—when more than one negative factor or behaviors intersect and intensify one another (e.g., a distracted driver encountering a careless pedestrian).

a. Intersectionality is the often unexplored element in analyzing the gravity of a situation. Such is the case in better understanding how different the plight is for those experiencing multidimensional poverty versus simple monetary deprivation (which, of course, is already tremendously trying).
b. Almost all things are plural. There is not a lone cause, but *causes*.

96

Actions intersect at three points:

- Someone's cumulative character.
- That individual's current emotional state.
- The thresholds or barriers presented by the immediate physical environment toward taking that action.

97

So much of the needless suffering that exists results from placing unrealistic demands on the world, pining for what should be rather than engaging with what actually is and making sure to give thanks for the times when things actually go the way that they "should."

98

We do not need to win every battle but to recognize that we are almost never even at war to begin with.

99

In a nutshell: conflict resolution is the release of tension in a nondestructive manner which is also sustainable. It does not lead to the return of the previous level of energy (or an increase), but brings greater balance and equilibrium.

Foster kindness, whenever possible, even if braving inhospitable terrain.

The father, the son, and the unholy ghost

My father was neither a pious man nor a fallen one.

He was both.

I loved him not because of but in spite of his flaws.

Regardless of his religiosity (or some might say because of it), he repeatedly cheated on my mother, who struggled against emotional fragility throughout her life.

But at the same time he adored her. His actions stemmed in part from his terror at the depth of his feelings toward her, a defensive reflex to create distance from her power over him and his own vulnerability.

They were married fifty-six years. He nearly went bankrupt providing care for her at home the last eight months of her life and held her hand as she died. After she passed, the resonance drained from his voice, never to return.

He was a devoted father, the sole breadwinner who also attempted to fill the parental void left by my mom's illness with the few hours he was spared from work. He'd lost his own mother suddenly at age eight. For him the most unthinkable act was leaving a child unparented.

He squared off with me menacingly twice—once when I was a teen and then again late in his life. We did not come to blows only due to my backing down—the first time out of fear, the second through volition. That final occasion, I chose to walk away because I valued more continuing to have a relationship with my father than "winning." After that incident, our bond grew stronger.

I fight the unconscious tendency to replicate the sins of my father—a warped way of keeping him present, a buffer between myself and mortality. The moral struggle is to instead maintain what was admirable in him while also unashamedly acknowledging his imperfections without demonizing or inadvertently reproducing his errors.

This constitutes a healthier way to honor him, and the sloppy complexity of life itself.

Though I'm not Jewish, I was recently subjected to an anti-Semitic attack. I live near the synagogue of a traditional Hebrew community. While walking in the neighborhood one afternoon, I crossed paths with a drunk woman in a mob of even more young drunk women. She charged me without prior interaction, ripped the hat off my head, and scolded, "You can't do things like this." She'd misinterpreted that my wide-brimmed, black hat signaled that I was a member of the local religious community.

I immediately thought of Rwanda and how during the 1994 genocide militants at roadblocks often had to consult the tribe listed on each person's national identity card to determine who should or should not be slaughtered. Many of my mother-in-law's family and friend's fates were determined this way.

The butchers weren't otherwise even sure who to hate. They only knew that they hated.

Ultimately, the target itself was arbitrary.

My sister, Jane, was born prematurely, with severe Down syndrome, a hole in her heart, and deaf in one ear. Drastically underweight and lacking a swallow reflex, the doctors sent her home to die. But she defied all expectations.

Throughout her life, Jane's vocabulary was limited to only a few dozen words.

She was not without anger, but its rare appearance was almost always measured. Nor did she like each person she met equally. Nonetheless, she remained a friend to all. Forgiveness was her forte.

When she smiled, there was a depth I've never seen otherwise except in people's most candid and intimate moments. There was no undertow to Jane's joy.

She acted as our guide, gently nudging us toward perspective:

Yes, life sucks. But there's beauty to be found just the same. And as fucked up as it is, it still could be so much worse.

Live without wallow.

Be thankful for this day.

Afterword

False claim: "There is no middle ground."
Reply: "It's all middle ground (... well, *almost* all, anyway)."

I know that I am not as outwardly peaceful a person now as when I was a teenager. This is not said in an exultant way. But recognition of this fact allows me to ongoingly invest toward more closely matching my intentions and actions.

I was raised to keep peace at all costs—even in the face of abuse, and most of all at my own expense. This was beneficial professionally in crisis arenas but disastrous personally. Unfortunately, martyrdom lends itself quite easily to many Irish Catholic boys. The path back from that to healthier and more bona fide behavior has been a treacherous one where the risk of going too far in overcompensation perpetually lurks—the trading of one imbalance for another.

These truths prevail:

It's hard to escalate in the presence of someone who is remaining calm. It is difficult to argue with someone who is agreeing with you. And it is damn near impossible to attack someone physically who is not there.

No, it's not "all good."

But it's *mostly* good with *some* people *some* of the time.

And though I don't necessarily like most individuals, I strive to have love for everyone.

Let's not doom ourselves with the curse, "Things couldn't be worse."

To those absolutists who overstate, "I don't have a racist bone in my body," the most appropriate rebuttal is that racism is not a known orthopedic condition.

Perpetually fear whoever claims that they are "not an angry person." They're likely one of the angriest motherfuckers you'll ever meet.

Rather than aspiring to greatness, aspire to goodness.

And when facing conflict, rather than vengeance let us seek to mend.

Overviews

BARE BONES
escalation management

30-second version:
Remain calm,
ask questions,
give options.

5-second version:
Stay silent, listen intently,
and nod (in agreement).

1-second version:
Run!

Three specific things to *do* in crisis

1. **VOCAL CONTROL:** Concentrate on regulating your voice.
    a. The voice function as the brakes in escalation, since vocal versus verbal expression is not usually under our conscious control.
2. **LISTEN SPECIFICALLY:** Listen to *who* a person is speaking about more than their volume or emotional state.
    a. Abusive individuals speak primarily about others ("you"). Merely angry individuals instead speak mostly about themselves ("I/me/my").
3. **SELECTIVE SPEECH:** Think before speaking by starting and structuring messages with nonpersonal pronouns ("It/that/what/this") rather than personal pronouns ("I/me/you").

Three Underlying Factors Found in Behavioral Crisis

1. **FEAR:** Be sensitized to the person's almost inevitably being threatened by what is happening.
   a. Threatening the individual will only heighten their existing fear.
2. **TRAUMA:** Unprocessed emotional wounds and trauma are the keystones of most negative conduct.
3. **PHYSICAL:** There are always physical factors (hunger, thirst, environmental cold or heat, defecation or urinary needs, intoxication, crowding or presence of an audience, bodily pain) contributing to or fueling an escalation.

   In short: Are they truly "bad" or is it just the blood sugar talking?

Let's get physical

1. Stand beside versus directly in front of someone.
    a. Use an open-door, sideways stance rather than a full-frontal one.
2. Never position yourself between two (or more) individuals.
3. Establish and maintain equality with the person vertically. If they are seated, sit. If they are standing, stand.
4. Force yourself to nod in agreement with the individual.
    a. This additionally helps prevent our locking-up into defensive postures (e.g., puffed chest, hardened glare, etc.).
5. Do not attempt to speak to someone who is more than six feet away. Under those circumstances, your voice will be raised and by default anyone in between will be made a part of the exchange.
    a. Bridge physical distances so that you are never too far (or too close) to someone when speaking.
6. Whenever possible try to move together with the person and change environment. Ideally, from indoors to outdoors or a smaller space to a larger one and, whenever possible, away from audiences.

Harmonizing values with intention

Five societal solutions:
1. Don't fetishize contrariness.
2. If occurring, halt the eroticization of vengeance.
   a. A tragic misconception is that violence is a solution to problems rather than a major cause of them.
3. Identify and address whenever overly simplistic and false dichotomies derail communication and specificity.
4. Confront informational narcissism—the conviction that whatever "I've heard" or learned is the authoritative and optimal information.
5. Work to expose and correct polarized statements and positions.
   a. Instead, persist in attempting to pinpoint the multilayered truth that exists along the spectrum between the oversimplification of either/or and all-or-nothing.

About the Author

For over thirty years—since 1993—Ian Brennan has successfully trained over one hundred thousand people across the USA (as well as Europe, Africa, Asia, and the Middle East) in violence prevention, anger management, and conflict resolution at shelters, schools, hospitals, clinics, jails, and drug-treatment programs, including such prestigious organizations as the Betty Ford Center, Bellevue Hospital (New York City), UC Berkeley, and the National Accademia of Science (Rome).

These trainings are based on over fifteen years' experience working as a mental health specialist in locked, acute-psychiatric settings, the job that's been rated "the most dangerous" for intentional injury in the state of California. From 1991 to 2001, he conducted psychiatric triage interviews in the county emergency room for Oakland, CA, one of the busiest in the country.

Additionally, he's worked throughout the United States providing one-on-one anger-management sessions for individuals facing criminal charges due to violent conduct, and, relatedly, provides expert testimony in such cases.

He is also the author of nine books, including *Anger Antidotes* (2011) and *Hate-less* (2014).

Additionally, Brennan is a Grammy-winning music producer who has worked with artists as diverse as Fugazi, country legend Merle Haggard, Sleater-Kinney, and filmmaker John Waters. Since 2010, he has produced over forty records by international artists across five continents (Africa, Europe, North and South America, Asia) which have resulted in the first widely released, original-music, local-language albums from many nations, among them Rwanda, Malawi, South Sudan, Azerbaijan, Bhutan, São Tomé, Comoros, Suriname, Romania, and Vietnam.

These musical projects have been spurred by his conviction that many of our societal problems could be lessened if we listened to each other more closely and democratically.

His work has been featured on the front page of the *New York Times*, on BBC World, PBS television, CNN Live, and in an Emmy-winning segment of *60 Minutes* with Anderson Cooper reporting.

ABOUT PM PRESS

PM Press is an independent, radical publisher
of critically necessary books for our tumultuous
times. Our aim is to deliver bold political ideas
and vital stories to all walks of life and arm the
dreamers to demand the impossible. Founded in
2007 by a small group of people with decades
of publishing, media, and organizing experience, we have sold millions
of copies of our books, most often one at a time, face to face. We're old
enough to know what we're doing and young enough to know what's at
stake. Join us to create a better world.

PM Press
PO Box 23912
Oakland, CA 94623
www.pmpress.org

PM Press in Europe
europe@pmpress.org
www.pmpress.org.uk

FRIENDS OF PM PRESS

These are indisputably momentous times—the financial system is melting down globally and the Empire is stumbling. Now more than ever there is a vital need for radical ideas.

In the many years since its founding—and on a mere shoestring—PM Press has risen to the formidable challenge of publishing and distributing knowledge and entertainment for the struggles ahead. With hundreds of releases to date, we have published an impressive and stimulating array of literature, art, music, politics, and culture. Using every available medium, we've succeeded in connecting those hungry for ideas and information to those putting them into practice.

Friends of PM allows you to directly help impact, amplify, and revitalize the discourse and actions of radical writers, filmmakers, and artists. It provides us with a stable foundation from which we can build upon our early successes and provides a much-needed subsidy for the materials that can't necessarily pay their own way. You can help make that happen—and receive every new title automatically delivered to your door once a month—by joining as a Friend of PM Press. And, we'll throw in a free T-shirt when you sign up.

Here are your options:

- **$30 a month** Get all books and pamphlets plus a 50% discount on all webstore purchases

- **$40 a month** Get all PM Press releases (including CDs and DVDs) plus a 50% discount on all webstore purchases

- **$100 a month** Superstar—Everything plus PM merchandise, free downloads, and a 50% discount on all webstore purchases

For those who can't afford $30 or more a month, we have **Sustainer Rates** at $15, $10 and $5. Sustainers get a free PM Press T-shirt and a 50% discount on all purchases from our website.

Your Visa or Mastercard will be billed once a month, until you tell us to stop. Or until our efforts succeed in bringing the revolution around. Or the financial meltdown of Capital makes plastic redundant. Whichever comes first.

Silenced by Sound: The Music Meritocracy Myth

Ian Brennan
with a Foreword by Tunde
Adebimpe

ISBN: 978-1-62963-703-7
$20.00   256 pages

Popular culture has woven itself into the social
fabric of our lives, penetrating people's homes
and haunting their psyches through images and earworm hooks. Justice,
at most levels, is something the average citizen may have little influence
upon, leaving us feeling helpless and complacent. But pop music is a
neglected arena where concrete change can occur—by exercising active
and thoughtful choices to reject the low-hanging, omnipresent corporate
fruit, we begin to rebalance the world, one engaged listener at a time.

Silenced by Sound: The Music Meritocracy Myth is a powerful exploration
of the challenges facing art, music, and media in the digital era. With his
fifth book, producer, activist, and author Ian Brennan delves deep into his
personal story to address the inequity of distribution in the arts globally.
Brennan challenges music industry tycoons by skillfully demonstrating
that there are millions of talented people around the world far more
gifted than the superstars for whom billions of dollars are spent to
promote the delusion that they have been blessed with unique genius.

We are invited to accompany the author on his travels, finding and
recording music from some of the world's most marginalized peoples.
In the breathtaking range of this book, our preconceived notions of art
are challenged by musicians from South Sudan to Kosovo, as Brennan
lucidly details his experiences recording music by the Tanzania Albinism
Collective, the Zomba Prison Project, a "witch camp" in Ghana, the
Vietnamese war veterans of Hanoi Masters, the Malawi Mouse Boys,
the Canary Island whistlers, genocide survivors in both Cambodia and
Rwanda, and more.

Silenced by Sound is defined by muscular, terse, and poetic verse, and
a nonlinear format rife with how-to tips and anecdotes. The narrative
is driven and made corporeal via the author's ongoing field-recording
chronicles, his memoir-like reveries, and the striking photographs that
accompany these projects.

After reading it, you'll never hear quite the same again.

Muse-Sick: a music manifesto in fifty-nine notes

Ian Brennan with a Foreword by John Waters

ISBN: 978-1-62963-909-3
$14.95   128 pages

Grammy-winning music producer Ian Brennan's seventh book, *Muse-Sick*, is a primer on how mass production and commercialization have corrupted the arts. Broken down into a series of core points and action plans, it expands upon Brennan's previous music missives, *Silenced by Sound: The Music Meritocracy Myth and How Music Dies (or Lives)*.

Popular culture has woven itself into the social fabric of our lives through images and earworm hooks. Justice, at most levels, is something one may have little influence upon, leaving us feeling helpless and complacent. But pop music is a neglected arena where concrete change can occur. By exercising active and thoughtful choices to reject the low-hanging, omnipresent commercialized and prepackaged fruit, we begin to rebalance the world, one engaged listener at a time.

In fifty-nine clear and concise points, Brennan reveals how corporate media has constricted local cultures and individual creativity, leading to a lack of diversity within "diversity." *Muse-Sick*'s narrative portions are driven and made corporeal via the author's ongoing field-recording chronicles of places including Comoros, Kosovo, Pakistan, and Rwanda, with disparate groups such as the Sheltered Workshop Singers, brought to life by Marilena Umuhoza Delli's striking photographs.

"*Ian Brennan's* Muse-Sick *is a passionate, thought-provoking chronicle of traveling beyond the mainstream to listen to unheard music created by the unsung.*"
—Maureen Mahon, NYU, author of *Right to Rock: The Black Rock Coalition and the Cultural Politics of Race and Black Diamond Queens*

"*We can never hear enough of the fresh, conscientious perspective of Ian Brennan. His words gives voice to people who have been silenced.*"
—Booker T. Jones, frontman of Booker T. and the M.G.'s and winner of the Grammy Lifetime Achievement Award

Missing Music: Voices from Where the Dirt Roads End

Ian Brennan with an Introduction
by Marilena Umuhoza Delli and
Foreword by Dame Evelyn Glennie

ISBN: 979-8-88744-037-8
$15.95   168 pages

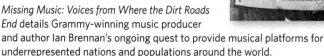

*Missing Music: Voices from Where the Dirt Roads
End* details Grammy-winning music producer
and author Ian Brennan's ongoing quest to provide musical platforms for
underrepresented nations and populations around the world.

In a compact and quick-read format, *Missing Music* collects the latest
narratives from Brennan's field-recording treks. This edition features
a greater emphasis on storytelling and an even greater abundance
of photos from his wife, Italian-Rwandan photographer/filmmaker
Marilena Umuhoza Delli.

Together, they meet the elderly shamans of the world's most musical
language, Taa, a tongue that sadly is dying, with fewer than 2,500
speakers left. The duo traveled the most remote roads of Botswana to
find the formally nomadic people now relegated to small desert towns.

In Azerbaijan, Brennan and Delli ascended to the mountainous Iranian
border to record centenarians in scattered villages of the Talysh minority,
where the world's oldest man reportedly reached the age of 168. The
result is the only record ever released to feature the voices of singers
over one-hundred years of age.

Among other tales, Brennan also updates the saga of the Sheltered
Workshop Singers following COVID, including the tragic deterioration of
his sister, Jane.

Arising from the more than forty records that Brennan has produced
over the past decade from underrepresented nations such as Comoros,
Djibouti, Romania, South Sudan, Suriname, and Cambodia, *Missing Music*
serves as the newest suite in the multiverse symphony of the world's
most ignored corners—the places where countries expire and the
"forgotten" live.

Ancestor Sounds - Africatown CD

Africatown, AL

Catalog No: PMA 025-2
$14.95   32 minutes

An album of landmark recordings featuring residents of the Africatown community, including descendants from the last slave ship brought to America, the *Clotilda*. This recording is meant as an impressionistic document rather than a definitive historical narrative. All recordings were performed on-site as 100% live first-takes. The outdoor nature of the recordings graphically renders the encroaching and ominous industrial sounds of the area. A combination of various folk traditions, the pieces on this album combine both historical narrative and contemporary life experiences for the people of the Africatown community. Intended as an audio companion to the book *Missing Music: Voices from Where the Dirt Roads End*, these recordings also stand strong on their own. Proceeds benefit the Africatown Drummers, LLC and various other local organizations.

Our Ancestors Swam to Shore CD

Africatown, AL

Catalog No: PMA 027-2
ISBN: 979-8-88744-099-6
$14.95   34 minutes

Our Ancestors Swam to Shore showcases the rarely heard music of Angolar Creole (N'golá) speakers from the African islands of São Tomé and Príncipe. Many of the five thousand residents are descendants of escaped Angolan slaves, who, as their folklore tells, swam to shore after a shipwreck off the coast. "Gola" has historically been used as a slur on São Tomé and its speakers are widely regarded as the lowest class; today, most work as fishermen. On *Our Ancestors Swam to Shore*, produced by GRAMMY-winner Ian Brennan and Italian-Rwandan filmmaker/photographer Marilena Umuhoza Dellias, the power of music goes beyond melody, harmony, and instrumentation and acts as a transcendent force to tell a people's history with a nod toward the future.

When to Talk and When to Fight: The Strategic Choice between Dialogue and Resistance

Rebecca Subar with Forewords by Esteban Kelly and Douglas Stone

ISBN: 978-1-62963-836-2
$20.00   208 pages

When to Talk and When to Fight is a conversation between talkers and fighters. It introduces a new language to enable negotiators and activists to argue and collaborate across different schools of thought and action. Weaving beautiful storytelling and clear analysis, this book maps the habits of change-makers, explaining why some groups choose dialogue and negotiation while others practice confrontation and resistance. Why do some groups seemingly always take an antagonistic approach, challenging authority and in some cases trying to tear down our systems and institutions? Why are other groups reluctant to raise their voices or take a stand, limiting themselves to conciliatory strategies? And why do some of us ask only the first question, while others ask only the second?

Threaded among examples of conflict, struggle, and change in organizations, communities, and society is the compelling personal story that led Subar to her community of practice at Dragonfly, advising leaders in social justice organizations on organizational and advocacy strategy. With lucid charts and graphs by Rosi Greenberg, *When to Talk and When to Fight* is a brilliant new way of talking about how we change the world. In his foreword, Douglas Stone, coauthor of the international best-seller *Difficult Conversations*, makes the case that negotiators need this language. In a separate foreword, Esteban Kelly, cofounder of AORTA Anti-Oppression Resource and Training Alliance, explains why radicals and progressives need it. If you are a change-maker, you will soon find yourself speaking this language. Be one of the first to learn it. Read this book.

Re:Imagining Change: How to Use Story-Based Strategy to Win Campaigns, Build Movements, and Change the World

Patrick Reinsborough & Doyle Canning

ISBN: 978-1-62963-384-8
$18.95   224 pages

Re:Imagining Change provides resources, theory, hands-on tools, and illuminating case studies for the next generation of innovative change-makers. This unique book explores how culture, media, memes, and narrative intertwine with social change strategies, and offers practical methods to amplify progressive causes in the popular culture.

Re:Imagining Change is an inspirational inside look at the trailblazing methodology developed by the Center for Story-based Strategy over fifteen years of their movement building partnerships. This practitioner's guide is an impassioned call to innovate our strategies for confronting the escalating social and ecological crises of the twenty-first century. This new, expanded second edition includes updated examples from the frontlines of social movements and provides the reader with easy-to-use tools to change the stories they care about most.

"All around us the old stories are failing, crumbling in the face of lived experience and scientific reality. But what stories will replace them? That is the subject of this crucial book: helping readers to tell irresistible stories about deep change—why it is needed and what it will look like. The Story-based Strategy team has been doing this critical work for fifteen years, training an entire generation in transformative communication. This updated edition of Re:Imagining Change *is a thrilling addition to the activist tool kit."*
—Naomi Klein, author of *This Changes Everything: Capitalism vs. the Climate*

"This powerful and useful book is an invitation to harness the transformative power of stories by examining social change strategy through the lens of narrative. Re:Imagining Change *is an essential resource to make efforts for fundamental social change more enticing, compelling, and effective. It's a potent how-to book for anyone working to create a better world."*
—Ilyse Hogue, president, NARAL Pro-Choice America